I0200611

Inspirational thoughts
by mark a. arcenas

copy right 2014

For Jessica Marie,

introduction proverb:

me: "Why one should NEVER commit suicide"

a friend: when the devil tempts you to hurt yourself he is preventing you
 From accomplishing something great, something great that God had In store for you, and also maybe that you will help other people. God had something planned for your life the moment eternity and creation was formed in his hands.
That' why the devil wants you to kill yourself, to prevent you from accomplishing and carrying
out God' will
God' will for you is not only for you it' also the people you will help that is linked to your will with others.

    my conversation with my friend

                You've heard of the Norwegian proverb "never argue with a drunk"well I say never ever argue with a mentally ill person they'll drive you crazy,,-me

a girl said to me,: "I'll kill myself and prove them wrong,

I replied: "No you'll prove yourself wrong, Don't kill your self then you'll prove them wrong and prove yourself right, Your stronger then this, you've been through worse,

the girl (crying) said " I don't matter anymore"

I said "yes, you do you matter, your future success matters, think about it when you become a doctor the people who made fun of you will be so mad and jealous, at how successful you will be, that they wished they never made fun of you in the first place. (she smiled and gave me a hug.)

When you save a life you, you didn't just saved one life, you saved a universe of generation of lives, you saved her future children, future husband, and future career, Failure to save a life, one life didn't just die, a countless generation of lives would never come into existence of you never saved that one life. So save a life if you can.

Do good, and good is rewarded back, if we do evil, evil is given back, we open ourselves to evil by doing evil, do good and good will triumph.

i have more respect to a person, I don't agree with then with someone who seems nice, but something else behind your back.

be good, and good will follow. - an eight year old homeless child.

you have to forgive, so you can live in peace,-me

"What love to thee, the lost to give,

Sadder still, dies the nightingale,
the stars cry out, her name, my heart in death,
a love I remember, so young goodbye,
a child in the mirror I see, I call her name,
I see the eternal night, O Lord, protect her what evil maybe,
for I can not hold her hand a ghost she must be.
In my pass she held my future, in the present God said she mustn't be.
O light , O light, send me your sword, that killed the child in me,.
I, who told her, "yes, someday you will be."
grief be this turn the dusk, at dawn who will rise. Not me
Her name God suppressed, O love her crown, O love I've lost.
O love the child sees in the mirror, love is lost.
What love to thee, the lost to give, sadder still dies the nightingale.
Her name, O blood of stars, upon the Heavens, painted the darken woe,
in that class room, where sunlight shown, and storm began, I promised her,
"She will be."her dream began, an angel I was sent, I love one such as thee.
She is the eternal rose, in the middle of that class room born, where Heaven Collided when Jessica Marie was Born.,
I a peasent not a knight, not a prince, I not a king, I a peasent not a god, yet I love her still.
O tears of the angel, the guardian from above, who set the sails of God, O lord, to her door, a promise I gave to thee, a kiss with a blood of red, O Lord, what light blinds me, from above, an angel of love, takes her away from me, O dream O dream, what stars did tell.
I will burn through hell, what love to thee, the lost to give,
sadder still dies the nightingale.

the black of death, I release her from his crows, sorrow is a child in me, who love her still.
Sorrow crowks the nightingale.

Her kiss of life that lives in me eternally, O light O light, that bleed the stars, making angels cry.
My name and hers not writtin in the immortal sky,

her name I gave to God, when I die, so ever safe she will always be. And happy with another man, a very rich man who isn't me."

Day 1

I' rather know the ugly truth then live in a beautiful lie.

Day 2

I have more respect to a person who insults me to my face then one who does it behind my back, because they aren't man enough to step up to you.

Day 3

Love and believe in yourself, then you'll make mountains move and accomplish your dreams

Day 4

Having faith during the trails and woes in the stages of your life is being guided by the invincible hand of God' providence.

Day 5

Faith is believing the unknown; I have faith that there is another day but I don' know if I'll be around to see it.

Day 6

Live life as if it had purpose, as if it had meaning;

Day 7

The four evils of this world are:
1) the Devil
2) the flesh
3)the self as a god as in self gain worldly power and wealth and self vain glory
4)the world's empty false promises-by Saint Thomas Aquinas

Day 8

A rich person doesn' need to tell others she or he is rich, just as wise a person don' boost about his or her wisdom.

Day 9

Conceited people only love themselves.-king Solomon

Day 10

with life there is nothing to fully understand, just live.

Day 11

Love is honesty a determined journey together by deed and a duty fulfilled by each person.

Day 12

 Love and life is more difficult in "real"life. Compared to movies and books

Day 13

There are two kinds of people in this world:
9) foolish people that know that they are life time learners
10)   and foolish people that deny that they are fools.

Day 14

Those that never learned about their mistakes are promised by the hand of Faith that it will be repeated.

Day 15

age is just a matter of mind, if you don't mind it, it don't matter.

Day 16

When ever you meet a new friend test their loyalty of that first
friendship before you can really trust her or him.-king Solomon

Day 17

Wisdom is more important then riches, after all your wisdom will
support your needs.
- King Solomon
Day 18

Don' hang around with wicked people they will not only teach you
how to sin but their malice will engulf you to the bottom of the
abyss.-king Solomon

Day 19

If a temptation is snaring you, offer it up to the Lord and stay away
from its arena.

Day 20

True love waits for marriage.- a religious woman said.

Day 21

Advise on whom to marry:
Dear child listen well, marry a homely girl. One who don't degrade
her body before the eyes of other men, one who is a homemaker, one
with good moral up bringing.
One who is soft heated but strong in trails. One who is not secular?
A dignified woman
Marry a woman who always listen to her mother and obeyed her

father.

With this in mind you'll go beyond your 65th wedding anniversary.- a religious woman said.

Day 22

Advise on friends:
Choosing a friend, I've learn that quality in a friend is better then quantity.

Day 23

When invited to dinner at a friend's house never be the first to serve yourself.
-King Solomon
Day 24

If you are troubled by a painful experienced memory, such as child abuse or any sorrowful weight upon your life. My advice is put all your pain and emotions in a box and crush it.

Day 25

Always have time for companionship with your grandparents you never know when they may not be around.

Day 26

Don't lose the one you love, to the one you like.

Day 27

You find a higher truth in faith, and a higher happiness in that philosophy.

Day 28
Some people think illnesses and disabilities limits us, but in reality

they don't. Our ailments encourage us to be strong because we can endure pains that healthy people can't.

Day 29

sometimes a person who is too, nice, says sweet compliments, just can't be trusted, they want you to let your guard down, so they can take advantage of you. don't trust such a person.

Day 30

Don' take happiness in other peoples misfortune for God can take away yours too as well.

Day 31

A poet is a painter of words, a constructor of beauty. One must see through the eyes of a poet to harvest a collection of beautiful colors that is found in poetry. What a poet sees
A painter paints. Words drift like stars popping out of the sky. A poet is a designer of love, he or she brings refreshing thoughts like cleansing water in the open mouth of a pen.

Day 32

What is the heart?

The heart is the deepest recesses of our lovable will. What and who we love we treasure it in our hearts.

Day 33

There are only three kinds of people that live life to the fullest; it' Saints, philosophers, and poets. They live each day as if it was their last and live as it has purpose, not only on their own behalf but on the service to their neighbor and how much they can help others, by putting others first.

Day 34
A person who is an expert in lying is an expert in destructive dishonesty.

Day 35
A person who criticizes too much about other people' accomplishments are people who wished they had accomplished.

Day 36

A person who takes celebration on other peoples suffering is a person who will suffer more then the person they are making fun off.

Day 37

Love is the mother of peace.

Day 38

Death is really the beginning of life. If you followed God's commandments you will save yourself and live.

Day 39

Don't lose your life and soul by making others difficult.

Day 40

A friend who stays with you, not to the end but stays with you always. Is wine lasting the test of eternity?

Day 41

There are only three words that define the meaning of life. "Jesus loves me"

Day 42

There are only three words that define; birth, life, death, Heaven, eternity-
"Jesus loves me"

Day 43

There are only five words that define Hell
" refuse to know Jesus Christ"
Meaning separated from my creator.

Day 44

There' only one word that define true lasting strong marriage
"Miracle"

Day 45

There' only one word that defines true love.
"Gift"

Day 46

There's only one meaning for long lost love, why a man can' be with the woman he loves

-to save you from an unhappy marriage.
-the bible

Day 47

There's only two reasons why you can' have children

Option reason 1: to save you from godless sinful children

Option reason 2: so you can adopt a child who needs to survive with your love and care and support.

Day 48

Take the advice of the good Lord, Jesus Christ.
Pray for those who hurt you everyday.

Accept nothing-

Blame no one-

Do something that pleases your father in heaven by loving Him, and your neighbor and yourself.

Day 49

There are many reasons why you can't sleep at night.

1. You didn't get what you want.

2. The sorrow of the pass is eating you a part until it consumes you.

3. Love left you.

4. You're an addict.

5. Worries, sorrows, broken hearted.

6. Someone broke an oath a very important promise to you.

7. You'e being oppressed.

8. Afraid, scared.

9You'e taken an innocent life.

10. Lonely.

11.Separated from loved ones.

12.Homeless

13.Your hurt, the list goes on and on.

Day 50

Fear not there is a remedy for sleepless nights.

1.faith in God
2.prayer
3.will

Day 51

Fear of God, the Lord Jesus Christ is the beginning of wisdom and knowledge,
Example I fear God so much that I don't want to offend him.

Day 52

When you love someone, the sun is brighter in their eyes. The other person is the stars and heavens of your paradise.

Day 53

A slap in the tongue is worse then a slap in the face.-king Solomon

Day 54

When you are close to God He will test you by evil that will come at you as angels of light.

Day 55

God' goodness will test you in the wisdom and virtue of humility.

Day 56

 Do good, good will follow, if you do bad, bad is given back.

Day 57

If your plans and ambitions never worked out, remember there are other things you can do, even better then what you had planed, far more rewarding then what you have always prayed for just do what you are already good at that someone else is not. - (my grandfather)

Day 58

Don't join in the mingling about with sinners and evil doers for you may share their faith.

Day 59

Silence that you return to an insulting tongue attacking you can save you from a useless argument.-King Solomon

Day 60

God' will for us is always better then our plans. Not only because we benefit from it here on earth but throughout eternity as well.

Day 61

Life can only be difficult if you make it difficult. So think life is easy, then it will be.

Day 62

If you love someone out of selfish pride, you only love yourself.

Day 63

If you love someone out of humility that' a gift from God.

Day 64

Fearing God is the most important thing you need in life, by doing so God will take care of you the rest of your life. -King Solomon

Day 65

God can only help you if you help yourself.

Day 66

Don't reject the gift of love by rejecting life.

Day 67

Absence of proof does not mean proof of absence.-Plato

Day 68

A person who is beautiful in the outside does not mean and can prove they are a beautiful
Person.

Day 69

Someone who is unattractive in the outside goes not mean they are ugly, inside they are more humble and lovely then most people who are conceited and take advantage of others with their looks.

Day 70

A wise person knows they know nothing, that they are life time learners.
A wise person knows sorrow and sadness will make them wiser. The more you observe the more you want to avoid the more you learn.

Day 71

Sometimes to know the truth is to know what we were not prepared for.

Day 72

To know oneself is to have humility the acceptance of oneself as is.

Day 73

To experience life without trails, and tribulations is to live without the worries, sorrows of the rain, you need the rain refreshing waters to grow in wisdom and strength, like a beautiful flower needs rain for growth. By growing like that we grow in wisdom.

Day 74

A world without pain is a world without love. Love heals our pains while pain teaches.
Just as a life without suffering is a life without love, and love heals that persons wounds and the wound of pain teaches that person to live and survive. Then heal and out live the pain.

Day 75

They let all the young men go to war so that the older guy can have all the girls. And maybe if you die in a war your wife or girlfriend will be nailing every guy you hate, Lol

Day 76

To forgive you must pray for love, to forget your hurt you must hope for peace.

Two virtues needed love and peace. Once acquired you can forgive, forget, forever, always. All the time with love. With meek and humble of heart by following the Divine Lord Jesus Christ if you can't forgive forget you will never have peace and happiness and never be free.

Day 77

It is in sufferings, trails, sadness, and tribulations that our virtue and graces are tested and passed. Once the virtue is obtained the strength of the person is revealed.

Day 78

Another meaning for long lost love, is to mold you for a better love with someone else so you can love someone else stronger, because the love you lost will only ruin you, believe me dear child this is the truth of the meaning of long lost love, it' meant to be lost and buried in the pass because that lost love will only ruin you and make you unhappy if you had it. So God arrange you to be with someone better, someone whose been prepared for you in eternity. While the lost love is only a mistake to practice you for the real deal God opened up for you.

Day 79

We find ourselves through our off springs, they are our immortality.

Day 80

Death is the beginning to see the result of our life, our grades. Whether we were a good student in life or not.

Day 81

A real friend is as rare as a winter rose, false friends hit you everywhere like fallen rain.

Day 82

Forgive, forget, forever, always, all the time with love and peace. Then Jesus will forgive; forget, forever always, all the time with love for your sins. If you forgive others Jesus will forgive you too. You can't forgive on your own you have to pray for it
So God will grant you that grace to forgive, remember what He said "with humans it is impossible but with God everything is Possible."

Day 83

If you forgive, you will live, if not you will have no rest. If you forget you will have peace of mind, if not you can' forget the eternal pain of hell.
 Forever, by forgiving forgetting, you will be happy forever, live forever, and be with God forever, by forgetting you forget your pain, forever
By Always, you will always be free always all the time.
By all the time with love, if you do you will never imprison yourself with hatred that blinds you.

Day 84
For some people true love is false love. For what was true about it was a mistake.

Day 85

Sometimes freedom can imprison you of what you know.

Day 88

Some women are as beautiful as a rose but her thrones will harm you, and some women are just thrones, no rose.

Day 89

In judgment day you will see yourself as God sees you. There will be a station of shame where we can die of our own shamefulness because of our sins, seeing how much we offended God. Judgment before God will be the greatest embarrassment combined to all earthly embarrassment.

Day 90

The eyes of God, is the window of everything, when we see the incarnate truth we see our purpose.

Day 91

Keeping silent can save you from embarrassment, but talking too much can also put you in a situation of embarrassment.

Day 92

Sometimes you have to love a hundred times before you find the right one.

Day 93

The truth can sometimes put you in a trap, or release you from a trap.

Day 94

Two things that the devil wants you to think,

1) He wants you to think he don't exist

2) He wants you to think he does exist.

Day 95

Turn your sorrowful eyes towards our Heavenly mother the Blessed Virgin Mary

Apply your will to Hers because Her will for you is also the will of God.

Day 96

A simple friend can stay with you until the end, until the end when they get what they want from you and leave you abandoned when things go wrong. But a real friend stays with you always not to get what they want from you and then leave you dry. This real friend of yours who stays with you always will always be there for you, for the two of you to share and always have a friendship. And this friendship is seldom found among normal folks, but I find this friendship with God and in him a lone. I trust.

Day 97

Keeping a secret from a friend is bad because you have already betrayed that trust.
Because a secret will always harm someone or more people.

Day 98

to young people, your young your success is yours for the taking, go for it. Only person who can stop you accomplishing your dreams is you.

Day 99

Bad things never happen to good people. Remember the songs of King David "wicked things happen to wicked people" It's bad things happening to bad people and good things always happen to the righteous and God praising people. Sinful things happen to sinners. Remember the bad that tested good people is like gold and silver heated by the pressure on fire . . . the fire of the bad omen will never out match the light of the good, once we are tested and the heat from this fire we become the results of a beautiful diamond. For God is the light of the good, He raises the good each time we fall. Bad

people are made by the separation of the good. The separation of the goat and the sheep.
But sometimes the bad people will become good, by the influence of good people.

Day 100
Age is just a stage in life the higher the number the higher the blessings.

Day 101

God allowed evil to exist in our world, after the fall in the Garden of Eden so good is learn and produced out of our fall. Which is sin? Before the fall we, our first parents Adam and Eve was so connected to God that their bodies glowed with celestial golden light a long with God' purity and Divinity that after the fall they saw themselves as beast and monsters by covering their bodies with animal skin. And that divine glow they had was darkened with sin. So God allowed evil to exist so something is learn with the fall to bring good out of evil.

Day 102

Some people who are successful and rich with their accomplishments tend to look down on people who aren't. And mock those who are trying to accomplish their dreams and some who end up successfully forget where they came from. Like if they came from a poor family. They too forget about the poor. This is a bad thing one should never forgot where you came from.

Day 103

Live each day of your life, as if it has purpose and find the meaning of that purpose,

Day 104

Age is just a matter of mind, if you don' mind it, it don' matter.

Day 105

Others fear death because of what way of pain will be produced in the death they might die from. But we should really fear death when God judges us to see ourselves in God' eyes when we committed those sins. To feel that guilt and shame of embarrassment when God ask us "give me one good reason why I should not condemn you for your sins."God can only be merciful to you if you were merciful to your neighbor. Follow that and he will be merciful to you.

Day 106

We see our continued life through the eyes of our grandchildren.

Day 107

Patience is not only a virtue it is a crown of glory the amount of time of your waiting will be out succeeded by the prize in the end.
- (my father)

Day 108

Honest Love is stronger then time, better then wealth and fame.

Day 109

The greatest love of all is God the Son waiting to embrace the world as he died on the cross.

Day 110

Love is a journey together with two people one man and one woman.

Day 111

Old age is the strength of years experience; youth has the strength of endurance to experience the many years a head of reaching old age.

Day 112

hanging around with wrong people, don't mean your a wrong person, your just there in the wrong crowd.

Day 113

Suffering strengthens you and builds you up to be strong and wise enough to with stand the pains of life.

Day 114

The way to teach and prevent children from crimes starts with grown-ups setting a good example.

Day 115
How to educate our children depends on how adults behave around them.

Day 116

A vicious parent one with a vice habit and attitude is a dark example to his or her children.

Day 117

A virtuous adult who sets a good example teaches a child how to live a virtuous life.

Day 118

One who degrades himself or herself lowers their value in other people' eyes.

Day 119

You can not judge what you do not understand. Because we are not who we are judging,
Unless we do understand who we are judging but judge justly. And leave the full measure of judgment on God's eyes

Day 120
What is the measure of true lasting unending love, well it is measureless because it is endless.

Day 121

Love is when you love someone and even if they do not love you. You still love them anyway regardless how many times they say they don't and they reject you. You will always love them and by doing that for that rest of your life you will survive in that love.

Day 122

there are three sides to everything, yours, mine and the truth,

Day 123

With regards to your parents, always respect them, if you don't respect your Father and Mother, your children won't respect you, and if you have no kids, life will be difficult for you.

Day 124

Faith is knowing in a belief that we don't really know. I have faith the sun will rise tomorrow but don' know if I myself will rise out of bed.

Day 125

To "now thy self"is to have and pray for the virtue of humility

Day 126

Real virtue, is honest innocent virtue, honest innocent virtue, is true virtue.

Day 127

The more you have knowledge the more you don' know. There are things still we need to know that haven't been revealed and discovered yet.

Day 128
When we die it is when we really are born and live.

Day 129

Faith is the force of light in the dark that we do not know it is there.
Example: I have faith there is a light to another day but I do not know if I will be
Around to see it.

Day 130

Those who remember what happened to them in the pass and not learn a lesson from it may be, just may be repeated until the lesson is learn and the mistake be avoided by the lesson of virtue learn from the memory that was experienced.

Day 131

About age:

Age is just the stage we are "in" our lives. As experience, memories, mistakes, lessons learn and our education in life our different stages of age in life that educates us. Our age strengthen us in wisdom, of ourselves. The age we see in the mirror may not match the virtue of the soul, but it' okay. it is the age of the person that reflects the well earned grace in a life time.

Day 132

Sometimes parents are not always right.

Day 133

When we say and think of Jesus Christ and Mama Mary, it makes us feel we are in Heaven because they are loving us giving us an example of love that can be found in Heaven.

Day 134

To have virtue, we must act in virtue, to love virtue we must live in virtue.

Day 135
Vengeance begets an emptiness of endless cycles of worthless vengeance. It' death killing death.

Day 136

There are many things you can do in life as a career, far more better then what you have had wanted and hoped in life .-(my grandpa)

Day 137

Is it better, not knowing then knowing a truth that disrupts us.

Day 138

Virgin Mother Mary you are the one, you gave us the Son.

Day 139

Life is difficult because we learn something we don' know.

Day 140

Bad events cursing ones life blesses you with lessons and teaches you to shrive for the light to pull you out of the dark.

Day 141

Faith is your compass in life.

Day 142

Life is a puzzle Jesus is the missing pieces.
(my father)

Day 143

Disabilities and being handicap strengthen the human spirit and makes our hearts wiser.

Day 144
The lessons and values we learn yesterday will prove to be a working instrument for today.

Day 145

There is nothing wrong with being rich, as long is you don't make it your god.

Day 146

someone told me "it is better to have children after you are married, because God have united man and woman together in the sacrament of marriage that way he will bless you with God fearing children and healthy offspring."

Day 147

It is better to be married to one beautiful person for the rest of your life then sleeping around staining yourself with sin. A single man, is a wondering person.

Day 148

Understand yourself, first before understanding others

Day 149

A wise child always listens to their father and obeys their mother.

Day 150

I think some people tend to think to wish reality should be what they had wanted, and deny what "it" really is. They make their fantasy into their "reality" and forget about the reality of the real "world" that they should be living in.

Day 151

Love at first sight is two souls interlocking together. Each realizing the worth of the other.

Day 152

True love is two twin souls exchanging energy of love in to each other, feeding each other with a love that is eternal.

Day 153

Experiencing a long lost love is like wondering blind in the night.

Day 154

The unseen can be noticed as well as the undetected.

Day 155

We humans seek truth to any subject, it' like looking out the window of everything we want to know and only have our thoughts reflected back at us.

Day 156

Or when we seek truth we look outside the widow of what we search for, and find fragments of faded thoughts

Day 157

Does humanity know enough of what it already know at the present moment. Would it make any difference if it did or didn't.

Day 158

Can we learn things without understanding it without having another person teaching us?
Example no one teaches a baby how to walk it just does. Is the baby influenced to learn how to walk because the grown ups are able to. Like if you speak Chinese around a baby you are watching over. Eventually it will learn that language. So do we learn by our environment and surroundings.

Day 159

How does a thought give ideas, as ideas about composing music?

Day 160

Can we build ideas without the process of a single thought?

Day 161

About things that are about to happen before they actually do, can they be prevented from happening before it actually does bound to happen.
-Boethius

Day 162

a true friend, is like treasure from Heaven, while false friends hit you everywhere like falling rain.

Day 163

Starting today I will be the Good Samaritan.

Day 164

A good person is a God fearing person.

Day 165

Many of us need to stop and listen to what God gives us each day and admire it.

Day 166

Each day when you wake up always thank God for being alive to see another day to see one of his plans for the day unfold before your eyes. Before your life.

Day 167

Never take the Lord God name' in vain.

Day 168

Correct those who take the Lord God' name in vain. By telling them God loves them.

Day 169

When you first see and know that person you are going to marry you see them through the eyes of a poet, you can describe their beauty in words like a poet would like a poet deeply heavenly in love. Because heaven wrote their name in your heart.

Day 170

The world' greatest success can lead to the worlds greatest misery while the world's greatest misery will always leads to the world's greatest success.

Day 171

Be happy with what you have, better then having nothing.

Day 172

Conceited people only love themselves, they seek self gaining glory.

Day 173

When you are in love and the other person who says they love you, test them on that oath if it is a love of truth.

Day 174

Always spoil your children with love but never spoil them with materialistic things.

Day 175

Never gain selfishness out of a friendship, but earn each others dignity and trust.

Day 176

There are many great movies about love, of remarkable love stories, that's what makes the movies great.

Day 177

A love courtship without holy courtship is a love that won't last; seem goes of a marriage without holy countenance will end in an unhappy marriage.

Day 178

Never take desire in poor people's misery, for God' wrath will crash down on you.

Day 179

Trust and honestly is hardly ever heard and practice in relationships, these days.

Day 180

Pray and love those who hurt you, only God can change a person, because God will work in the person to change.

Day 181

A prayer shouting and crying in the heart of a person is a prayer heard in the heart of God.

Day 182

To understand and appreciate love and beauty you must see through the eyes of a poet, and have the heart of an angel.

Day 183

Home is where the family is not in a big mansion.

Day 184   .

Save your money, when things are going well, save your money when things aren't

Day 185

A good friend is always there for you, they don't count for the wrongs and the fights you've had with them, rather they cherish the love.

Day 186

Ever hear that saying: "things happen for a reason", well things also don't happen for a reason and God knows the reason why.

Day 187

We not only see with external eyes and the eyes of the mind, we also see with the eyes of the heart the reveal-er of beauty.

Day 188

Be a good example to children, because when you do your a hero before their eyes.

Day 189

A child is the closest to that of an angel

Day 190

True Love has no time

Day 191

Never wait for a promise that wasn't written as an oath.

Day 192

We all have ambitions and goals but God has the final say of what blessing we receive.
- King Sirach, who was King Solomon's little brother from the bible

Day 193

God loves you

Day 194

When the devil comes knocking at your door, just ask Jesus and Mary to answer it.

Day 195

Don' be merciful to the unmerciful. God is the same.

Day 196

Don't think of physical beauty as kindness, as something clean and pure and don't be too friendly with them for you don't know what really lies inside.

Day 197

As we age, we grow, and we learn, we get better. So happy birthday.

Day 198

The six mysteries of woman are, as follows:

1)She is afraid of aging old that she may lose her youthful beauty. But through her husbands eyes she is forever beautiful

2)She is afraid it maybe to late to have a child.

3)a mothers love

4)She wants to mother the child of the man she loves.

5) A woman' secrets and a mother's instinct.

6) she wants to give her virginity to the man she loves.

Day 199

What is better having lots of wealth, or being very wise yet still knows how to acquire wealth through your wisdom.

Day 200

Wisdom is the greatest treasure you can have, better then silver and gold.
-King Solomon

Day 201

You can't change the pass, but you can learn from it and you can change the future from becoming what you don't it want to become.

Day 202

The image of a person reflects his or her thoughts; example a person' fear is his or her strength to defeat what they can not face.

Day 201
The greatest improvement can lead to the greatest down fall, and the greatest downfall can lead to a great improvement.

Day 204

In each success there is always an opposite failure of probability.

Day 205

The must beautiful girl physically can always have a darker side that her external beauty cannot match.

Day 206

Sin is a disease that plagues the human race, and many do not even know they are infected by it. An invincible force that can be defeated by knowing its knowledge and it's opposite and it is Jesus Christ.

Day 207

There is some knowledge that is sometimes not a good thing to know. Because what we may know will harm us and ruin our innocence, if we can't handle it.

Day 208

Children are the greatest thinkers.

Day 209

a painter is a poet, a poet is a painter of words.

Day 210

it's a beautiful day today, match it with your beautiful life. Live it Beautifully

Day 211

What is in the heart, is what the soul desires. That God Grants to a prayerful person.

Day 212

Everything is vain righteous in this world- King Solomon.

Day 213

Don't talk about your plans, man, just do it. don't just do your plans, but succeed them.

Day 214

We all have, a gift of perfection in us. Use yours wisely and you will succeed at whatever you end up doing.

Day 215

Love God and neighbor, and you'll have more blessings and virtue from God's hands.

Day 216

A worldly rich person is a rich person in other people's eyes but to God's they are just a person-   Saint Alphonsus Liguori

Day 217

When a person is born time is the greatest enemy that person has.

Day 218

Don' lose yourself over something that can be replaced not worth dying for.

Day 219

When a humble person cries over a prayer, God listens and answer in his time, he answer's our prayers.

Day 220

Never marry someone or love someone if that person manipulates you and deceives.

Day 221

Silence can be a smart weapon against a shouting tongue.

Day 222

Humility the father of all virtues and the beginning journey to blessedness and gain acceptance and salvation in God's sight

Day 223

Give love to get love

Day 224

Forgive so you will be forgiven and free from that chain.

Day 225

If you laugh at other people's misfortune no one will help you when you reach rock bottom with your misfortunes, and your misfortunes will be worse.

Day 226

A woman's heart have to be so engulfed in God so when a man must know
God first before finding her and loving her- unknown.

Day 227

In order for a person to be courageous God gives that person a
chance to be courageous.
-Saint Alphonsus Liguori

Day 228

Even though we can not see God and the Blessed Virgin Mother
Mary, loving them
With all our hearts gives us an example of being with them in
Heaven.

Day 229

Can your unborn children forgive you for not marrying the woman
you love?

Day 230

Love is a gift of peace.

Day 231
Patience is a virtue for example: God put you in that station in a
situation in the current time of your life because that's where he had
placed you where you need to be. So you can benefit from it and the
people God placed in your life will help you shape your future.

Day 232

The priest is the sign and the instrument of God's merciful love for
the sinner. He is the instrument of the power which belongs to God a

lone; the forgiveness of sins the confessor is God's servant.
-unknown

Day 233

If you love somebody let them go, for if they return they were
always yours, and if they don' they never were.- Kahlil Gibran, the
heart of the matter.

Day 234

My friend look at life more and more seriously everyday and when
you do you will see
Things unfold before your eyes.

Day 235

Faith is stronger then doubt and love is harder then hate-
-Our Lady of Fatima
William Thomas Walsh

Day 236

Having a bible in your hands and reading it, I began to think this
bible is my direction in my life's travels. My true teacher, when I
read this, God's wisdom, power is here in my hands as I read this,
reading the bible cleanses the dirt in my mind.

Day 237
Every time when we sin we choose something that's not Jesus. Sin is
a spiritual disease,
give all my sins to the priest as an instrument to forgive me of my
sins.

Day 238
About suicide: a person is God's temple, and God's spirit lives in

you. God will destroy those who destroys God's temple, meaning if you hurt yourself you are hurting God.
Look it up in- 1 Corinthians 3:16-18 you get your answers there.
note: not all suicides go to hell, mentally ill people who commit it, go to heaven, because the illness over powered that person, it was the illness that killed the person.

Day 239
The blessed Virgin Mary is the fire, and Jesus is the light, the Blessed Virgin Mary is the veins Jesus is the blood, the Blessed Virgin Mary is the breathe Jesus is the life, Mary has the road map and she is the aid Jesus is the way. Mary is the Queen of Heaven Jesus is the King.

Day 240

About Spiritual Discernment if you feel inner peace and humbleness about what you are discerning then it is from the Holy Spirit.

Day 241

King Solomon wrote the book of Ecclesiastes
-according to Saint Alphonsus Liguori

Day 242

If you injure another and think you can get away with it, remember God will punish you 2 to 3 times over for that offense.

Day 243

Never ever under estimate the wisdom of the poor.

Day 244

Children obey your parents for when you have kids of your own, how well you obeyed to your parents will reflect back upon how your kids will obey you, when you become a parent your children should obey you.

Day 245

Never ever under estimate the strength of the poor.

Day 246

The young should marvel at the wisdom and experience of the elderly and the elderly should be amazed at the opportunity of the young.

Day 247

Real men don't hit women and children and the elderly.

Day 248

A real husband should love his wife and children.

Day 249

Real men don't fight for no stupid reason, like if someone dogs you, real men fight to protect their family and protect life.-

Day 250
Death to the just is only the beginning of life.-the bible

Day 251
Death to the wicked is death and suffering for good.

Day 252

Love someone who gave their love to you and willing to sacrifice.

Day 253

The elderly is what to the young a mirror of their future selves.

Day 254
When you found something that' not yours, return it to the owner for God will reward you with his blessings.

Day 255

A memory of long passed is a friend forever.

Day 256

A foolish person ask others about his or her mistakes, about the inner mysteries
Of life while a wise person ask the inner thoughts and voice inside their being.

Day 257
Love knows no waiting in time when you love someone.

Day 258
If you misbehave and gave your parents trouble and heartache in the same way your children will give trouble and heartache and disobedience.

Day 258
Never ever hurt a child for that child will never forget the harm you've done.
And scare them for life.

Day 259

We will know our true worth, when God Judges us on judgment day.

Day 260
I have heard a priest say that some of our dreams that we see and experience while we are a sleep is the work of the Holy Spirit. Will,

some dreams

Day 261
Before you say something harsh and crushing to someone especially
to someone who' a friend think about it how it will affect them and
your friendship. Harmful words will hurt and attack the heart while a
physical one heals. Because an insult on the tongue has a thousand
needles, causing a thousand hurts.

Day 262
A broken heart can drown in sadness. Scientifically it can. When a
person' so heart broken water will pump in the heart valves and dry
the person out with blood like how Jesus died on the cross, the
sadness will drown the sufferer.

Day 263
How do you make sense out of sadness, and sorrow, by uniting it
with God's suffering on the cross. Because by doing so God's
wisdom is united to ours gives us an understanding of his love. So
we learn to suffer out of love for love. And by doing so we find love
in our own suffering, and solace in our sadness. besides we heal out
of sadness we become stronger. We also will be victorious, because
God is also victorious

Day 264
What are friends without being a friend to yourself first.

Day 265
If you throw away your work, all you have worked hard for you
throw away.

Day 266
When you wake-up every morning say a sample prayer: Lord this
day I commend to you my spirit and thy will be done.

Day 267
When we want something so badly from God, and it is our desires to
have what we desire, but God don't answer it, and He gives us
something better more rewarding then what we originally desired.

Then we know God knows what's best for us.

Day 268

when you get sick, don't say, I'm sick, say I will heal and recover.

Day 269
The life and plans God gives was already arrange by providence as one of the missing pieces of His divine plan.

Day 270
The greater the sin the greater the mercy- Jesus Christ.

Day 271
By surrendering everything to God, let the flame of His Love melt you completely and allow Him to shape you any way pleasing to him.

Day 272
The most important step you can take to getting what you want out of life is actually deciding what that something is,

all of us when we die we're all going to wonder did i live enough, and love enough, or love to the most of my ability that i died loving that person. (figure of speech)

when i finally found that love of my life I'll feel like I've dead and be so happy that u gave birth to a new love. like being born and dying at the same time.

when u love this person u say i may not have seen the entire world country by country but, in their eyes i am the world and the universe is a country of joy in each moment u die and come out a live each time u look into their eyes.

and when we have problems it's good to finally meet the person humble enough to care and listen and advise us, and we get happy when they help us laugh our way out of our pit falls.

and u say thanks for Ur time listening to me, and being there.

Day 273

the Greek philosopher ask a very important ???

"KNOW THYSELF"

If u know yourself, the object of your knowledge is either yourself or something else; if the object of your knowledge is something other then yourself, then u do not know yourself. But if the object of your knowledge is yourself, then both the one knowing and the thing known are your self. If the image of your self is impressed upon your self , then it is yourself which is the knowledge.- Beothus

Day 274
God is a necessary being, that he is one, and that the universe is brought into being from Him and has resulted from His Being?- unknown source.

Day 275

Most friends are only your friends if things are going well, fake friends want to share in your glory, real friends stay with you regardless things are well or not.

Day 276

Some religious people, are self righteous, they look down on sinners, and have a holier then thou mentally.

Day 277

sometimes the most religious person isn't always the most holy person.

Day 278

Don't be too relying for your parents or spouse for money especially if they are rich, you need to make of yourself so you can stand on your own. Because they can run out dry. So make a living for yourself.

Day 279

While enjoying your youth always respect your elders, visit and spend time with your grandparents, your friends will always be there, your grandparents can go anytime.

Day 280

Be kind to others and kindness is given back with a blessing.

Day 281
Beauty , true beauty is not the physical appearance of a person it' in the personal character traits of the individual.

Day 282

A high tempered person is an idiot who does and says things without thinking and later learns he or she has embarrassed themselves, by doing silly actions out of anger.

Day 283

People who don' have patience are likely to be high tempered.

Day 284

Wanting to be famous and popular are for those who are conceited.

Day 285

Conceited and proud people seek to be praised and honored. While the unpopular and the no body' are the humble.

Day 286

A wise person answers his or her own deep questions in the stillness of their hearts.

Day 287

A wise person had to be a fool first in order to be wise to learn he/she was a fool.

Day 288

A wise person teaches himself or herself with the lesson they learn, while a fool takes no regard of it.

Day 289

People who manipulate and deceive think they are wise but in reality they are lairs and fools who deny that they are lairs and fools rubbing others out their innocence.

Day 290

Live life, as if it has meaning, because you are the meaning of your life.

Day 291

Only an idiot would allow themselves to be bribed by anyone who has money.

Day 292

Children are the greatest teachers of an adult, the adult seeing the child' treasure that the adult once had, the loss of their innocence.

Day 293

Epiphany experience

a few yrs. ago. on good Friday, i eat at a McDonald's restaurant and I'm having 2 fish sandwiches and an old man who also was having a fish sandwich now this old man i discerned that he was a christian catholic, and i seat across from him. we'e the only two costumers in the McDonald's restaurant. and I see and i discern that the old man was a very, very, sad and broken person, we were minding our own business when we make eye contact and he notice i have no wedding ring in my finger and i see he don' also. and i think to myself. Man, look at him I'd hate it if i end up like this old man, it' like i symbolizes his younger self who suffers from a long lost love like him & i feared i would be like him when I'm old. who never really lived loving someone throughout his entire life. This sad old man he probably experience a long lost love and out lived his brothers and sisters and his parents, and i saw the dying sadness on him, a lifetime of brokenness. and he was ready to finish on living and die what he never experienced as a human being who lived and loved, had a family and had lots of grandchildren, b/c he had always wanted that, and he was a prisoner of a misfortune, a prisoner of his own making from a long lost love he decided he couldn' let go. and he had the choice to move on and be with another woman a better woman who would complete him and love him in a manner that the long lost love he had couldn' promise him. i thought and say to myself i petty this old man. and pray for him. he was so empty and so sad sitting by himself, a lone in his life . and he sees a young man like me and he may have thought and said to himself, man this kid has a life time ahead of him i pitty him and feel sorry for him if he ends up like me, a lone throughout his sorry life and never got married and love someone.

Day 294

a wise woman told me this analogy

Girls are like
apples on trees. The best
ones are at the top of the tree.
The boys don't want to reach for
the good ones because they are afraid
of falling and getting hurt. Instead, they
just get the rotten apples from the ground
that aren't as good, but easy. So the apples
at the top think something is wrong with
them, when in reality, they're amazing.
They just have to wait for the right
boy to come along, the one
who's brave enough

to climb
all the way
to the top
of the tree.

Thoughts on this, analogy, the girls who are rotten apples, aren't really rotten apples, life's circumstances put them there, maybe they were abused as a child, Believe me I know girls whom society labels them as rotten apples, street walker, etc. etc. these girls have been so hurt starting early on in life, that when I talked to them, they would say "I will let this man, or woman hurt me do bad things to me, and I'm okay with it, because I can't cry anymore." these girls I've known some where place under human trafficking, yes, human trafficking. they have been so hurt all their lives that men and woman abuse them in the worse way that they became the pain and became the hurt that they can't cry anymore. People who have been in human trafficking say the most horrifying stories you could hear, "Ice cream trucks are used to transport the organs of people who are victims of human trafficking." someone told me. "sometimes truck drivers are bribed to transport underage victims of human trafficking." just because a girl is labeled as a rotten apple, it don't mean they are rotten, they were hurt by others, don't mean no one will ever love them.. There's someone for everyone. Well I'll tell you, God loves these girls who are called rotten apples,

Day 295

For I know well the plans I have in mind for you, says the LORD, plans for your welfare, not for woe! plans to give you a future full of hope.
When you call me, when you go to pray to me, I will listen to you.
When you look for me, you will find me. Yes, when you seek me with all your heart (Jeremiah 29:11-13

Day 296

the Greek philosopher ask a very important ???

" KNOW THYSELF"

if u know yourself, the object of your knowledge is either
yourself or something else; if the object of your knowledge is
something other then yourself, then u do not know yourself.
But if the object of your knowledge is yourself, then both the
one knowing and the thing known are your self. IF the image
of your self is impressed upon your self , then it is yourself
which is the knowledge.

Day 297

God is a necessary being, that he is one, and that the universe
is brought into being from Him and has resulted from His
being.

Day 298

have u heard of the native American proverb that says:

can Ur children forgive u for not marrying their mother,

in metaphysical speaking it means, if i never married the woman i love our children would have never been born and if they were never born can they forgive us for not giving them life.
I know It's deep

Day 299

forget about the ppl in ur pass there's a reason why they didn't make to ur future –unknown

Day 300
pain and sorrow is like

pain and sorrow is relieved when tears go down. it over comes the weight of our woe. it expresses our needs and strengthens us to carry our cross, tears are the pain and blood of the soul. but coming from a child who suffers so much, that child has gained true suffering and w/ that suffering comes true wisdom. it is said true wisdom can only be gain by true suffering

Day 301

in love.

some woman are as beautiful as a rose but her thrones will harm you. while some woman are just thrones very rarely you'll marry one who is all rose and no thrones.

don't lose the one u love to the one u like.

Day 302

there are 2 kinds of ppl in this world

1) wise ppl that say they are fools
2) foolish ppl that think they are wise.-Socartes
there are 2 kind s of ppl in this world
1)wise people that admit they know nothing
2) foolish people that deny they are fools.-

Day 303

we see beautiful love stories in movies played by actors and
actresses, yet sometimes we wished we are living those lives
these actors are playing.

Day 304

the greatest success in the world can lead to the greatest
misery in the world. while the greatest misery can lead to the
greatest success.

Day 305

what is a man or woman to gain profit of the world and
lose their soul- Jesus Christ.

Day 306

remember God can make a poor person rich in an instant as he can make a rich person poor w/ a wave of his hand.

Day 307

long lost love.

why a man can't be with the woman he loves, is to save him from unhappy marriage. b/c if they had children they may be in danger.

Day 308

life;

life can be difficult if we make it so.

Day 309

life is difficult because we are in this womb called the universe once we die and are born out of this womb we will truly live.

Day 310

if a child died a horrible death, remember God took him/her home to heaven to save it from a sorrow if had it lived longer. -The Saints

Day 311

real wisdom comes from real suffering real suffering comes from real wisdom.

Day 312

it is in great temptation that a person's virtue is tested, if the temptation is past the virtue is earned.

Day 313

never ever underestimate the wisdom of the poor-
Day 314

the greatest humiliation can lead to the greatest honor while the highest honor can lead to the greatest humiliation.

Day 315

God said Love thy neighbor, because He wants you to love what he loves.-the Saints

Day 316

good and bad angels

philosophy by mark arcenas

God don't exist in time not in eternity. But He exist in and out of what he creates, we are in eternity when we die & go to Heaven. God exist out of it, yet he is a part of eternity and outside of what He created it, out of eternal time and has total control of what he creates.

now Good angels and bad ones jump in and out of our 3rd dimensional worlds as well as ghost and passed away spirits, for beings like a ghost is a type of purgatory purgatury is latin for "Puritying stage" according of the Saints experience and testimony, in order for us to see them the good and bad angels they must slow down in movement manipulate time and space. and fit into our reality. that's why if u see one good or bad angels u get a sense of void that time slows down. Same thing when we see ghost that ghost seems faded in visional, they are fade like fog because they are in the dimensional world above ours so they must create a rift in the dimensional time streams thus slowing down time for us to see them.

When we see bad or good angels you are aging while the angel good or bad are ageless can not age, that is why they try to fit into our reality and imagination. and has one half of it's being in their dimensional world in the 4th or the 5th, and other half in the time and space in our dimensions the 3rd. that is how they communicate to us by slowly very slowly jumping back and forth into our dimensional world slowing down time.

when u see good angels, you get a small sample of Heaven a small pocket in time and space & Heaven and eternity was opened up, and it effects you in a Celestial manner that's why you can't think of an evil thought. Regardless how hard you tried. and the effects only last as long as your in the vicinity of the good Angels presence.

God is the energy flow that keeps the separate dimensional worlds open.

they came in the form we are attracted to the bad angels do. It knows your desires. two things the devil or his devils know and want from you. The devil want u to think he does exist and he wants you also to think he don't exist. the Saint's say the Devil is a master of lies. Read how he tempted the first woman he psychologized her.

the devil tempts us,
he wants to make you think that the evil tempted on you is a good and a desirable thing,

he knows your weakness, but it only knows half of your strength which is God. if you redirect your weakness with your strength Say "in the name of Jesus The Lord what do u want" the enemy will confess and is unable to lie, because you invoke on Jesus.

it obliviously wants your soul but it BELONGS to GOD.

i hope this educates u all about the good Angels and the Bad.

Day 317

There's no greater wound then the wound you get from your first love.

Day 318

when you laugh at someone because they are being embarrassed, remember you will be laughed at also ten times worse, in return when you get embarrassed because that's how karma works.

Day 319

Eternity last forever when you love someone.

Day 320

Me: your scared of dogs you must be a chicken, you'e a chicken because your scared of dogs.

My four year old niece: I' not a chicken uncle Mark, I'm a little girl.

Day 321

My niece: do it for the children uncle Mark.

Day 322

My six year old nephew: the next time you see me I'll be a lot smarter

Day 323

My youngest niece: uncle mark I don' want you to go to college, because I'll miss you.

My oldest niece says to her little sister: but if uncle Mark don't go to college, he'd be stupid,

My youngest niece responds: I'd rather want uncle Mark to be stupid then for him to go away to college and me miss him.

Day 324

God answer prayers faster and in more effective if we fast for what we pray for.
Because we are giving something up sacrificing for what we are asking God.

Day 325

Suffering can merit Heaven, because there is no salvation without suffering.

Day 326

If your spouse or girlfriend or boyfriend cheats on you my advise is never ever take them back, because by cheating on you they may have contacted a sexually transmitted disease and by doing so and taking them back they'll infect you and your unborn child with the disease, and they'll cheat on you again and leave you, leaving you to rise your child alone on your own.

Day 327

About fighting with your spouse or better half, if you feel guilty after the fight and want to say your sorry and apologize be the first to say sorry, if you don't you don't love this person. And they'll know it.

Day 328

When you pray for a dying person like a loved one, you must pray not for what you want for that person, but most importantly pray for what the dying person wants, whether they want recovery and heal from the illness and live or stop suffering and return and go home to the Creator and die in this world only to be born and live forever in the next. You must accept the dying person' prayers to die naturally even if they are suffering never ever unplug their life support because we are not suppose to go against God wish for the person, they may be suffering but they are gaining it for the Kingdom. If you unplug a dying person's life support against their will and against God' will, you will pay dearly when you stand in judgment before the high most your creator. Because what you did to the dying person God will do to you. And if a dying person wants to die by having the life support unplugged never give them that, assisted suicide is going against God's will and God's will is not respected and carried out.

Day 329

Enjoy your day, today, love and accept everything that happens today. it's your day.

Day 330

Live today, as if you will succeed in your goals, and at the end of the day, you have succeeded your goals.

Day 331

Can my unborn children forgive me for not marrying their mother, meaning if I never married the girl I love it would mean me and her would never have children together
And if we never had children together can they forgive us for not giving them life.

Day 332

If you want something from God even if it' wrong for you and you don't see it that way, and want it anyway, sometimes, though not always God will give it to you to make you see it was wrong for you to be asking for something that would hurt you, and when God gives it to you God will work in your soul to help you to realized its wrong and you'll give it up. And know that God was right by not granting your prayer in the first place, and once you'll notice that you'll be more obedient to God's will and acceptable to his plans for you. And you'll have confidence in God hands in him molding your life. And have complete trust in what He does for you. Because it is His will that is done now on earth as it is in Heaven. Everything has an eternal effect. Even the actions you don't take or fail to do.

Day 333

What you do in you life be it evil or good it always has an eternal effect onward. And the people you hurt or love and do good to, eternity sees it. And it effects them and you eternally also .

Day 334

I believe, I strongly believe when we die God will let us see, the choices we made and the choices we didn't make, the things that didn't happened compared to the things and events that did and how we could have learned from them and how it could have shaped us and our lives and our character. the cause and effect of every choice we didn' make God will give us the knowledge of what could have been.

Day 335

Every girl I met I was attracted to could have been the one.

Day 336

Be careful what you pray for because what we ask from God comes with a price, we won't know it until we get what we want. Everything comes with a price my child your salvation has been paid for by a very heavy price, the death of God was what we paid for your salvation He died for your sins so that you may remain innocent before the most High because we offend Him by our sins, because of God' Son Jesus took the blame for us.

Day 337

God is not your own personal Genie. You don't pray to God to get, to always get what you want, you pray to God because your suppose to love him. And honor God who created you out of nothing, who created you out of love.

Day 338

When you love someone, and you can't be with that person, and love them anyway, you are hurting, because you love this person. Love is painful. It wouldn't be love if it wasn't painful.

Day 339

Think about the person you have loved all you life, and think about how much you love this person, that you are willing to die for them you love this person more then you love and care about your life. Now think about putting this person in a situation, In a very difficult situation where you put them in danger that it would cost them their life, having loved this person you are willing to have them die and you always love them regardless what happens. Now imagine putting this person in a horrifying death that would cause torture that would lend to their death, all because so they could save other people. Think about having them be put to torture and death before your eyes just so you can save other peoples' life. Having them die for another. That's what God did for us, He allowed His only Son to be put to torture that lend to his death just to save you. He let his son die for you.

Day 340

There is no love without sacrifice.

Day 341

Don't ask someone to do something, that you yourself won't do.

Day 342

You don' get married for that sake of getting married, you get married because you love this person.

Day 343

Sometimes silence is better then from someone who talks too, much,

Day 344

Human Judgment is misunderstanding, because sometimes our judgment on others isn't what the other person really is.

Day 345

Nothing in our power, not the devil or all the fury in hell, or even the created cosmos, no created being can ever, ever obstruct the Holy Will of God from being carried out.

Day 346

Sometimes the religious person, isn't always the most holy person.

Day 347

Think happy thoughts, and happy things will happen today.

Day 348

Do all things with love and faith, So the things you do will succeed.

Day 349

With regards to power, how fair does one go with so much power.

Day 350

Mentally ill people are not who they really are, it's when they are cured is the real self being revealed.

Day 351

Today i will over come my goals.

Day 352

A person's true strength is shown when they forgive and forget.

Day 353

Can the people in Heaven, visit the people who are in Hell?

Day 354

Never give up praying for good can only come out of Prayer

Day 355

Sometimes we have to make mistakes, to see how wise we grow out of it.

Day 356

We suffer terrible trails, because we don't understand ourselves we do evil things to others and because of it that evil reflects back at us because we have harmed others.

Day 357

The rich people that die and go to Heaven will have the same sadness that poor people had and went through while they were rich on earth.

Day 358

Sometimes the best way to help someone is the scare them so they won't do anything they regret.

Day 359

sometimes it's okay to fail, good will come out of it, when you try again.

Day 360

If you do not love your neighbor you are not in the path to Holiness

Day 361

moments of miracle happens everyday. your living one now, your alive.

Day 362

respect your elders, they have suffered more then you, have been around more then you, respect your elders.

Day 363

If you made mistakes in your life, keep moving foreword and soon you'll notice your future accomplishments are greater then your mistakes.

Day 364

keep believing in your goals, because soon you'll be living it.

Day 365

 We suffer because we love, that's what happens when you love someone, we suffer because there is no love without suffering, suffering is the result of loving someone to death, like Jesus died for us, out of His love for us, so that we may be innocent before His offended Father, in Heaven so Jesus took the blame for us, because He loves us. Remember suffering teaches us, while love heals us. There is no suffering that love can not heal.

www.ingramcontent.com/pod-product-compliance
Lightning Source LLC
Chambersburg PA
CBHW051045030426
42339CB00006B/212